Praise for *There Are Trans People Here*

"The declarative premise of this collection, that there are trans people here—in the bookstore, in history, on the bus, 'next to you,' wherever you are—should not need to be said. Yet, in the cis imagination, trans life is so often understood as figural, as less than fully here. Given this, H. Melt's matter-of-fact, precise, cartographic poems perform necessary care work for the trans people and places they attend to and yearn toward. Deeply grounded in the plain, bountiful fact of trans worlds—and insisting on our worlds to come—this book offers all who need it a map to a world 'forever in bloom.'"

—Cameron Awkward-Rich, author of *Dispatch*

"*There Are Trans People Here* is an ode to trans joy, resilience, and communal care. A trans-utopian manifesto for a world that 'let[s] us be beautiful / on our own terms.' H. Melt's verse is bold, stark, and uncompromising. Threading elements of familial narrative, memoir, and queer history, they trace through-lines from our past to a brighter, queerer future."

—torrin a. greathouse, author of *Wound from the Mouth of a Wound*

"In *There Are Trans People Here*, H. Melt celebrates the blooming of trans identities and experiences in a landscape often hostile to trans survival. By invoking self-determination and communal care, these poems meld individual resilience with collective resistance to illuminate the everyday beauty of trans lives in refusing the lure of conditional inclusion to instead challenge dominant institutions of oppression, demand structural change, and remake the world."

—Mattilda Bernstein Sycamore, author of *The Freezer Door*

"*There Are Trans People Here* is a book that straddles the lines between past, present, and future, looking back in order to imagine what is new, and in the imagining, makes it possible, brings the future to us in a way that is touchable, right there, alive and under our fingertips. In the poem 'City of Trans Liberation' H. Melt writes, 'Where there are no borders / between who we were / & who we are / becoming.' For we are always becoming, always dissolving borders, or else, erecting them. In these poems H. Melt dissolves and becomes and becomes."

—Fatimah Asghar, author of *If They Come for Us*

"Reading this book it is abundantly clear that H. Melt is not only a brilliant poet but also a diligent reader. These poems pay homage to poets in H. Melt's lineage, while also giving us vibrant portraits of their community and envisioning a future world where safety, freedom, joy, and love for trans people is not only possible but abundant and right here."

—Jamila Woods, singer and songwriter of *LEGACY! LEGACY!*

THERE ARE TRANS PEOPLE HERE

H. MELT

Haymarket Books
Chicago, Illinois

Published in 2021 by
Haymarket Books
P.O. Box 180165
Chicago, IL 60618
773-583-7884

www.haymarketbooks.org
info@haymarketbooks.org

ISBN: 978-1-64259-572-7

Distributed to the trade in the US through Consortium Book Sales and
Distribution (www.cbsd.com) and internationally through Ingram
Publisher Services International (www.ingramcontent.com).

This book was published with the generous support of
Lannan Foundation and Wallace Action Fund.

Special discounts are available for bulk purchases by organizations and
institutions. Please email info@haymarketbooks.org for more information.

Cover design by River Kerstetter. Cover background and interior collages
from "Transgender Hiroes" promotional broadside, MOTHA, 2013. Courtesy
of Chris E. Vargas.

Library of Congress Cataloging-in-Publication data is available.

Entered into digitial printing November, 2021.

Dedicated to my trans ancestors, elders,
and mentors who show me what's possible

"Care is deeply political."
—Hil Malatino, *Trans Care*

TABLE OF CONTENTS

THERE ARE TRANS PEOPLE HERE

THERE ARE TRANS PEOPLE HERE

after Jamaal May

There are trans people here
so many trans people here
is what I am trying to say.

When they say we are all
trapped in the wrong body
impostor, impossible. No.

We are on the bus
next to you. In the
cubicle next to you.
In the check out line
next to you.

Some of us are sex workers
teachers, artists, nurses
homeless, unemployed
& hungry too.

We are as real
& complicated
as anyone else.

But they won't stop murdering.
Stop legislating. Stop imprisoning.
Stop claiming we are ruining our
countries, families, friendships
& futures too.

When every day
we awaken to
build them
anew.

ON MY WAY TO LIBERATION

for Pa Howie

I'm on the train
wearing a pink shirt
with a floral tie

on the way to celebrate
my grandfather's liberation
from dachau

when the nazis
came for his family
in Kovno, Lithuania

my grandfather
dressed like a girl
to stay close to his
mother & sisters

when he immigrated
to the united states
he changed his name
from *Michelson* to *Melton*

I've changed my name
& my clothes too
on my way to
liberation.

ALL THE MISSING SWEETNESS

Forgive me for crying & screaming
in my bedroom, refusing to pile into the car
making us late for every high holiday service
forgive me for stepping on my neighbor's toes
as we found four seats in the synagogue together
forgive me & I'll forgive you
for forcing me into a skirt
not paying attention when I didn't
break the fast, for eating apples raw
without dipping them in honey first
which I now squeeze into my cup
every morning, trying to recover
all the missing sweetness
from every passing year.

DYSPHORIA IS NOT MY NAME

after Ross Gay

Joy brought me here.
Lifted me onto this bed
on wheels, tied drawstrings
behind the back of my gown
affixed a hairnet atop my crown.

Look, in this country alone, there are
millions of us, *naturally occurring*
sweet things, with names
we carved ourselves.

No matter what the doctors say
I castrated myself & I'm all smiles.
There are so many surgeries
I could've had but timing
is everything.

It's a new decade, a new life.
Purple is the color of my scars.
Purple is my favorite color.
I'm forever in bloom.

TRANS CARE

When I went to the
feminist health clinic
I said hysterectomy

they said iud, didn't mention
misoprostol or that a pharmacist
would ask, *are you pregnant*?

they said insertion will only
take a few minutes, slight
cramping may occur

nothing about metal rods
puking up my breakfast
or suicidal ideation

after Sylvie survived
her surgery, I knew
I could too

I gathered the letters
I fought with insurance
I wrote a care plan

River watched
The Price is Right
with me in pre-op

Logan got me a unicorn balloon
& slept soundly as my catheter
was slowly removed

Sam drove me home
from the hospital &
picked up my pills

Eve organized my meal train
Jamila & Fati ordered fried chicken
Dominique bottled hibiscus lemonade

Ruby & I shared a pesto pizza
Emily cooked a veggie quiche
Fred delivered vienna beef

my dad sent a gift basket
my mom cooked mac & cheese
Ydalmi came with me to post-op

my iud is history
my tubes are finally tied
my uterus & cervix gone

this is not birth
control for me, it is
a beginning.

TO SYLVIE, TO FRANK

after Frank O'Hara

I wish I was having a coke with you
maybe a cherry, though I prefer
orange crush, apple juice, or iced tea
I would drink out of the bottle with you

on Coney Island, atop the Wonder Wheel
on Lake Michigan in a leather jacket
on Lake Champlain or my ikea couch
which you called "T Girl friendly"
with your long legs, your hands
picked up my call, when
a truck almost ended me

in Chicago, it is 6:48 pm
in Los Angeles it is 4:48 pm
I'm texting you in the middle
of a writing workshop, in the middle
of a pandemic, which stopped us
from being together & Frank says
the only thing to do is simply continue
I do not want to continue
without you.

AT THE CHICAGO MARATHON

a woman drapes
the canadian flag
over a barricade

I dangle
the trans flag
& she asks

what country is that?

when Logan
rounds the corner
with his sister
by his side

I hand him the trans flag

he wraps it around
his new chest
like a cape

as he flies
through the city
beaming with pride.

INTENSIVE CARE

River woke up
with their name
on the whiteboard

a crucifix on the wall
their parents straight
from New Mexico

we talk of poems
of estrogen, who
sent the flowers

when the nurse
asks me to shave
their face, I do

when the nurse
slips a *she* in
my direction

I don't correct him
River does, despite the
difficulty of speaking

I wish we woke up
in a different world
but we're here

holding hands
in intensive
care.

GIOVANNI'S ROOM

Est. 1973

is many rooms, many floors, a couple
winding staircases, new & used books
records & clothes, a chandelier with
its namesake book behind glass
a leather section, where I find
a chainmail necklace for ten dollars
a poetry section, where I find myself
Jamila & Raquel, this is for us
the oldest gay bookstore in
the country raises a trans flag
above the street, raises money
for AIDS & who better
to aid us than our own.

IF YOU ARE OVER CIS PEOPLE

after Morgan Parker

Don't kill yourself.
Make trans friends.
Schedule an appointment at
Chicago Women's Health Center.

Don't watch or listen to fox news.
Search for Janet Mock's writing
on the internet or the shelves at
Bluestockings or Unabridged.

Don't stay at a transphobic job
or apologize when you are
misgendered or misnamed
by family or friends.

Don't go home
for the holidays.
Cook your own feast.
Set your own table.

Use the bathroom
when you need it.
Don't hold it in.

FAGGOT WITH FLOWERS

In the summertime
I walk to the farmers market
on my lunch break from work

most of the vendors are queer
selling tomatoes & peaches
empanadas, cider & curds

I spy brain flowers, which my mom
occasionally bought, though
she favored gladiolas

I debate whether or not
to buy flowers, they are
not food, a bit of a luxury

as I walk back to work
proudly holding
my cockscombs

a man in a grey pickup truck
blows a stop sign, presses
the gas in my path

he cracks the window
to yell faggot at me
missing my body

I go home & place
my flowers in water
on the kitchen table

trying to forget
what will die
in a few days
time.

TO ALL THOSE LISTENING

*From the way the general description of the apartment
has been provided me, some items may not be "suitable
for viewing" by the public at-large, especially any minor
children which would possibly accompany their parents.*
—**A. Steve Warnelis**, Property Manager, XL Properties

When I found the letter
hung with blue tape
on my front door
I ran outside

My girlfriend
waiting in the car
to take me away
from my home

I couldn't sleep
in my own bed, eat in my
own kitchen, ride the train
without thoughts of jumping

My apartment walls
said *no hetero*
said *buttfuck the binary*
said *I am alive*

My family said *medicate*
said *history of depression*
said *this isn't discrimination*
My lawyer says *illegal*

My therapist says *trauma*
I say *help* & I say *thanks*
to all those listening
answering my calls.

AT THE DREAM JOB

after Carmen Maria Machado

I am surrounded by books
I meet my favorite authors
I listen to friends read poems
I hosted my first book launch
I started out at minimum wage
the owners call the cops
my coworkers are mostly white
men call about licking my pussy
women harass me for sex repeatedly
I am told you are erasing lesbians
I am told this is a feminist workplace
I am told your pronouns are a joke
where I am a joke, a trans person
working at a feminist bookstore.

ODE TO TERFs

you are not trans
radical or feminist.
you are exclusionary.

you say
back in my day.
back in your day
you denied our
existence.

you could read
Stryker's *Transgender History.*
Research us in the ONE archives.
Visit Monica Helm's flag in the
Smithsonian. Watch *Free CeCe
Disclosure* or *Southern Exposure.*

you cite the transsexual empire
spell *women* incorrectly
hijack pride parades
& mourn michfest.

we are living
in a new world.
you can join us
or become
extinct.

MEETING CHELSEA MANNING

After the Lambda Literary Awards

In manhattan, I'm bored
at an after party, the dj is bad
no one is dancing & only
the vodka is free

I notice poets sitting
in the corner: Sam &
Franny & Cam & William
tells me Chelsea is here
I don't believe him
but it's true

there's a circle around her
the host Mx. Justin Vivian Bond
the lawyer Chase Strangio
the journalist from vogue
the documentary filmmaker

I introduce myself
as a writer & ask
what she read
in solitary

I don't know this is
her first night out
since release

I already know, we've both
read *Nevada*, both lived
in Chicago & considered suicide
like most trans people, I know.

TRANS LIT

after Jamila Woods

Trans Lit is bullshit unless it is written
by trans people, unless it is written
for trans people. I want Trans Lit
that breaks linear narrative.
I want Trans Lit to bash back
against the police. I want Trans Lit
to take up an entire bookshelf
in the library. I want Trans Lit
in every classroom, in every backpack,
in every pair of hands on a long commute.
I want Trans Lit not to be a federal crime.[1]
I want Trans Lit in prisons, to set my
brothers, sisters & siblings free.

---

1 In 2015, Chelsea Manning was facing solitary confinement, partially due to a "prohibited property" charge related to books and magazines that were confiscated from her cell, including Casey Plett's book *A Safe Girl to Love.*

CITY OF TRANS LIBERATION

after Martín Espada

Where statues
of Lou & Sylvia
dance in the streets

Where no kids are
kicked out or run
away from home

Where no body
asks for ID or
our *real* names

Where every body
has a body
they believe in

Where we can go
outside in the daytime
without being harassed

Where we are taught
to love instead of kill
ourselves

Where Trans Day of Remembrance
celebrates those who died
of natural causes

Where there are no borders
between who we were
& who we are

Becoming.

ON TRANS STREET

on trans street
everyone knows
your chosen name

on trans street
there are bungalows
courtyard buildings
& rent control

on trans street
there are bike lanes
abundant wheelchair ramps
& prompt snow removal

on trans street
there is free STI & HIV testing
doctors prescribe hormones
& perform abortions
without a fight

on trans street
there is a school where
trans history is taught
by trans teachers

on trans street
there is a mural
of Miss Major
at Stonewall

on trans street
Juliana Huxtable
is the resident dj

on trans street
no TERFs
are allowed

on trans street
no catcalling
is allowed

on trans street
there are
no prisons
no checkpoints
no police stations
no military bases
no detention centers

on trans street
the cemetery
is always full
of visitors

on trans street
we are never
alone.

AT TRANS HOUSE

there is a garden
where berries &
sunflowers grow

in the backyard
kids learn how to swim
in suits that fit them

everyone cooks
or cleans in the
kitchen together

in the basement
there is a dungeon
& a dance floor

the neighbors are
not afraid to leave
a spare key

when a fuse blows
or the toilet overflows
we know how to fix it

light fills the living room
where comfy couches
allow us to finally relax.

TAKE ME TO THE TRANS SPA

where I can get my nails done
with my mom, without
toxic chemicals

let me change
in the locker room
soak in the jacuzzi tub
cool down in the pool
with a strawberry daiquiri

let me sweat in the sauna
& in the back room where
glory holes are filled
with fingers

let there be deep tissue
massages, drag bingo
on mondays, clothing
swaps on tuesdays

let there be a hair salon
sliding scale electrolysis
& lavender shampoo

let there be eyeliner tutorials
tips on beard trimming
& preventing hair loss

let there be an abundance
of ferns, aloe plants for
soothing scars &
a weeping willow

outside our doors
let us be beautiful
on our own terms.

CAMP TRANS

At camp trans
no cis children
are allowed

cabins aren't separated
by gender, instead
they are named
after riots:

Stonewall
Compton
& Dewey

the dining hall serves
Cooper's Donuts
for dessert

Jennicet Gutiérrez leads
a workshop on making
protest signs

Chris Mosier guides
campers on bike rides
through the woods

Kye Allums coaches
basketball drills
on dribbling
& defense

Jiz Lee reads
Sex Is a Funny Word
aloud as the crowd
roasts marshmallows

Laura Jane Grace
plays guitar around
the campfire & lulls
everyone to sleep

in the morning
the ghost of Billy Tipton
blows sweet sounds
over the intercom as
we continue to rise.

TRANS MUSEUM

At the trans museum
admission is free
for trans people

trans students rush
off the bus, excited
for their first visit

every artist on the wall
is trans, every curator
& employee is trans

the bathrooms are blessed
with good lighting & ample
period products

the cafeteria is full
of foods high in
phytoestrogens

the gift shop sells
binders, chokers
flags & gaffs

the auditorium hosts
packed readings with trans
poets from around the globe

the archive is open
to the public, ensuring
we will never disappear
.

EVERY DAY IS A TRANS DAY

Whether it's raining
or snowing, midnight
or awaking from a nap
working an eight-hour shift
or watching reruns, buying
groceries or folding laundry
celebrating a birthday or
burying a friend, lighting
a candle or taking a bath
calling mom or cleaning
the kitchen, mixing paint
or cookie dough, waiting
for bread or the sun to rise
every day is a trans day.

TRANS DAY OF REVENGE

after G.L.O.S.S.

on trans day of revenge
cis people will come out as cis
use the wrong restroom, be called
by the wrong name, lose a job
for being cis, be the only cis
in the family, fail to pass as cis
never feel cis enough

on trans day of revenge
all books about cis people
will disappear, cis characters
will be played by trans actors
the news will only talk about
trans people, the train will be
crowded with trans workers

on trans day of revenge
playgrounds will be full
of trans children laughing
learning & loving
isn't that the best
revenge.

I DON'T WANT A TRANS PRESIDENT

I want trans doctors
performing my surgery
trans journalists reporting
the news, trans historians writing
textbooks. I don't want trans capitalists
walking on wall street or trans cops
patrolling my neighborhood. I want
trans musicians playing on my stereo
trans designers crafting my clothes
trans chefs filling my stomach
trans farmers planting my food
& trans gardeners picking
flowers for my funeral.

TRANS PEOPLE AGAINST BANS, WALLS & BORDERS

When news of the Muslim ban broke
protestors fled to airports to free
people being detained & deported

Chelsea called & I took the red line
to the blue line to O'Hare
to international arrivals

lawyers hunched over laptops
& scribbled on yellow legal pads
in the dining area of a mcdonalds

I saw cardboard signs
made out of ikea boxes
& held one reading

trans people
against bans
walls borders

we surrounded police
we sat down on the streets
we removed the american flag
& put it back upside down

I want to travel
to a world where
no one needs papers
or government approval

to visit friends & family
attend school & work
to return or build
a new home.

& AGAIN & AGAIN

The Illinois Holocaust Museum was born
after nazis tried to march in Skokie
home to more survivors than
anywhere in the country

my dad took me
to the museum
the day after 45
was elected

I saw the signs

Warsaw: 1943
Skokie: 1978
america: 2016

the agents, the cages
the camps, the curfews
the fences, the fires
the gases, the guns

protestors held signs reading
fight anti-semitism & racism
unite against fascism
smash the nazis
& never again

THE MOST DANGEROUS JEW IN GERMANY[2]

was gay. Magnus Hirschfeld
established the Institute for
Sexual Science in Berlin

a hybrid
health clinic
& lecture hall
library & archive
proving we exist

in 1933
nazis burned
Hirshfeld's books
in the month of May

he fled the country
never to return for
the rest of his days

in the decades since
we've rebuilt what
was lost in the fire:

---

2   This is how hitler referred to Magnus Hirschfeld.

Affinity Affirmations
BreakOUT! Full Spectrum
On the Move Open Arms
Outreach True Colors
Youth Outlook Youth Seen

Callen-Lorde Hetrick-Martin
Lyon-Martin Thornhill Lopez
Whitman-Walker William Way

Have a Gay Day

Gay City
Magic City

Casa Ruby Proud Haven Unity House
The Attic The Living Room The Loft

We Are Family

TRANS TEMPLE

Build it & we will sing
together, rise together
sway & clap with parents
& partners & friends as
sun shines through stained
glass windows, we sip
wine & grape juice. we light
candles. we send money
in the tzedakah box
to Palestine. we skip
birthright. we cover
ourselves as we wish.
we let the torah fall
without punishment.
we repair & repair
& repair.

PRAYER FOR MY TRANS SIBLINGS

Praised are you who remember
Leelah & Blake, Greyson
& Mark, Layleen & Leslie

Praised are you who hold up
the trans universe, who
agitate & educate
migrate & radiate

Praised are you who shelter us
in libraries & nursing homes
locker rooms & train cars
prison cells & hospital beds

Praised are you who clothe us
in combat boots & leggings
button ups & chainmail
leather & pleather
faux fur & sequins

Praised are you who share
our joy in naming & renaming
screaming & dreaming
injecting & rejecting

Praised are you who soothe us
from the harms we inflict on
ourselves & each other

Let us hope for a day
when we no longer
need to pray for
our safety.

THE RIOTS MUST CONTINUE

For my 29th birthday, I went to Philadelphia
where my grandparents met at Temple University
& my great aunt was a docent at the art museum
& my great grandmother lived by Rittenhouse Square

which I visit in the rain, walking under my
purple umbrella, pausing at the fountain
reading off my phone, Philly's first
pride parade began right here

I walk a block to Dewey's Diner
to visit my trancestors
who were denied service
& arrested here in 1965

my nana lived so close
she could've heard the protests
or waved to me from her window

as River snapped a picture of me
in front of the bronze plaque
where Dewey's previously sat

now it is a construction site
most of my relatives are gone
but the marches & the sit-ins
& the riots must continue.

AFTERWORD

Writing this book challenged me to center trans joy. I am a lot more familiar with writing about grief. Most of the trans literature I've read focuses on the pain, discrimination, and violence trans people experience. Which is understandable, because our realities can be bleak. I've written about many of those moments in my own life. It was what I needed at the time. Now, I need trans joy. I need to know trans joy exists in order to imagine myself living in the future.

I remember the first time I picked up Nan Goldin's photography book *The Other Side*. It documents many of her trans and gender nonconforming friends at a drag bar in 1970s Boston. I found the book sitting on the shelf at a trans friend's apartment in Los Angeles. When I spotted the book and pulled it down, I opened a portal to the trans past. I was moved by the introduction, which states: "the pictures in this book are not of people suffering gender dysphoria but rather expressing gender euphoria."[3] I didn't know gender euphoria was possible. I knew that trans joy existed, but it was difficult to find. In those photographs, I recognized the deep joy of trans friendship through a historical lens.

While *The Other Side* gave me a glimpse at trans history, another book of photographs gifted me a vision of my future. The collection *To Survive on This Shore* by Jess T. Dugan and Vanessa Fabbre features portraits and interviews with trans elders from across the United States. On the cover is Mama Gloria, posing in the middle of a snowy Chicago street in a full-length fur coat. Inside the book, I found more trans elders who I recognize, know, and love. Flipping through its pages, I was able to imagine my future as a trans person for the first time. Reading *To Survive on This Shore* inspired me to write towards trans futures. It inspired me to organize an event with local trans elders who were featured in the book. At that event, I began to understand that I

---

3   Bea Rogers, Joey Gabriel, Sunny Suits, and Nan Goldin (Photographer), *The Other Side*, (Göttingen: Steidl, 2019), 7.

shouldn't only mourn the queer and trans elders lost to us. It is equally important for me to honor my elders who are still here. My future was no longer unimaginable. This opened up so many possibilities in my poetry because my focus expanded beyond surviving my day-to-day life. Finally, I could dream.

Transness is inherently futuristic. It requires us to imagine ourselves anew. At the same time, gender nonconformity has a long history that is often hidden, erased, and ignored by white supremacy, colonialism, and Christianity in the United States. While it may seem contradictory, writing about trans futures encouraged me to conduct historical and familial research. This is evident in poems like "On My Way to Liberation" and "The Riots Must Continue," where I merge my familial and trans ancestries. I am tracing my own lineage, one that embraces trans beauty, brilliance, and resistance.

There Are Trans People Here is also deeply connected to my experiences in queer and trans communities in Chicago. There are people working every day to make the world more welcoming to trans people. Many people I know are organizing to abolish the carceral state, stop deportations, defund the police, and decriminalize sex work. We are reimagining our communities one garden, march, protest, lesson plan, name change, and poster at a time. Trans people deserve to live long and fulfilling lives. We deserve a world free of prisons, police, and deportations, a world where we have universal healthcare and stable housing, and schools that affirm trans youth. Abolition and liberation are not abstract concepts. I know all of these things are possible because they are already happening.

My radical imagination was crucial in writing this book. Mariame Kaba writes in *We Do This 'Til We Free Us*, "My friend, scholar and activist Erica Meiners says that liberation under oppression is unthinkable by design. . . Our charge is to make imagining liberation under oppression completely thinkable."[4] I hope that my work makes trans liberation more thinkable and more of a concrete reality. In "City of Trans Liberation," I dreamt of public art dedicated to trans elders. Other people must've imagined this too. A few years after writing that poem, She Built NYC announced plans to install permanent statues of Sylvia Rivera and Marsha P. Johnson in New York. When I learned about this, it was a reminder that dreaming and action are both required to transform the world.

The artists, activists, and organizers around me encourage me to tap into my radical imagination, and create art relevant to social movements. They have paved the way for my own path to liberation. Art, writing, and creativity have always guided me into the future. *There Are Trans People Here* is my attempt to write the future I want into existence.

---

4 Mariame Kaba, *We Do This 'Til We Free Us* (Chicago: Haymarket Books, 2021), 92.

STUDY GUIDE

Written by Rabiya Kassam-Clay

Rabiya Kassam-Clay has a Masters of Education in Secondary Education with a focus in Social Studies from the University of Pennsylvania. She has taught middle and high school English and Social Studies in Philadelphia, Mexico City, and Los Angeles.

The full guide, with additional classroom activities, assessments, and resources, can be found online at www.haymarketbooks.org /books/1761-there-are-trans-people-here.

I. Three Big Questions

What is liberation? How do we recognize it? How do we practice it?

How does care work flourish in the context of community?

Who are our ancestors? What do our inherited and chosen ancestors teach us?

II. Analytical Projects

1. Imagine you were creating your own collage inspired by the one in the book. Locate a photograph that you would include in your collage of community. Take note of the visual elements present including: setting, objects, people. Determine the significance of the photograph: Why does it matter to you/us? What has or has not changed since the photograph was taken? What does it reveal about our past, present, or future?

2. Explore the themes of death and the future in *There Are Trans People Here*. In the afterword, H. Melt writes, "I need to know trans joy exists in order to imagine myself living in the future," and "Transness is inherently futuristic. It requires us to imagine ourselves anew." What is the relationship between death and the future?

3. How does H. Melt open up the theme of family? What are the connections and contrasts between families of origin and chosen families? How are different types of families in the book tied to sweetness?

III. Creative Projects

1. Who in your life has a story that connects to the poems in *There Are Trans People Here?* Listen to, watch, or read an interview from an oral history project. Examples include: the Act Up Oral History Project (and the corresponding film *United in Anger*), the Dragon Fruit Project, the podcast *Gender Reveal*, Outwords, and the

Tretter Transgender Oral History Project. Record an oral history with someone in your life like a friend, a relative, or a community member. Share it with text, drawings, audio, or video.

2. Create an artifact of abolition, liberation, or community care. As H. Melt writes in the afterword, "We are reimagining our communities one garden, march, protest, lesson plan, name change, and poster at a time." What would your poster or flag be? Consider the following resources:

> Monica Helms' transgender pride flag
>
> Trans Day of Resilience Art Project
>
> Aram Han Sifuentes's the Protest Banner Lending Library
>
> Justseeds' Celebrate People's History poster series
>
> Matthew Riemer & Leighton Brown's @lgbt_history Instagram archive
>
> ONE Archives Foundation's digital collection of posters

3. In the afterword, H. Melt writes,

> "In 'City of Trans Liberation,' I dreamt of public art dedicated to trans elders. Other people must've imagined this too. A few years after writing that poem, She Built NYC announced plans to install permanent statues of Sylvia Rivera and Marsha P. Johnson in New York. When I learned about this, it was a reminder that dreaming and action are both required to transform the world."

What other people and events in history do you think should be commemorated and how? What event, exhibit, museum, monument, public space, organization, or public resource do you think should be created to honor them? Create your vision.

IV. PEOPLE

Howard Melton, grandfather of H. Melt, was born in Lithuania in 1931. He was 10 years old when World War II began. Howard and his family were sent to a labor camp in Latvia. Howard's younger sister was sent on to Auschwitz where she was killed. His mother and older sister were both killed in Stutthof. Howard was sent to Dachau concentration camp where he survived countless human atrocities, including a death march at the end of the war. He moved to New York City in 1949, and later to Milwaukee to be near his close friend Al Beder, who he met in the camps. He was married in 1951 to Evelyn Melton. They had four children together, and eventually many grandchildren and great grandchildren. He's dedicated his life to speaking about his experiences as a Holocaust survivor. "On My Way to Liberation," p. 3.

Lou Sullivan (1951–91) was an HIV+ gay trans man who grew up in Milwaukee and moved to San Francisco in the 1970s. He was an activist, writer, and organizer, known for leading support groups for trans men, writing the newsletter *FTM International*, and helping found the GLBT Historical Society. During his time, trans people were often denied medical services by gender clinics if they were not straight. "Trans men weren't supposed to be gay. . . . In the eyes of the medical establishment, he could either be a man or attracted to men, but not both. Lou knew otherwise." You can learn more about Sullivan from the book *We Both Laughed in Pleasure: The Selected Diaries of Lou Sullivan* edited by Ellis Martin and Zach Ozma. "City of Trans Liberation," p. 26.

Marsha P. Johnson (1945–1992) and **Sylvia Rivera** (1951–2002) were friends, part of the Stonewall Riots and co-founders of Street Transvestite Action Revolutionaries (STAR) which provided housing and support for homeless queer and trans youth. Marsha "Pay It No Mind" Johnson was known for her joyous flower crowns, caring personality, and ongoing activism. You can learn more about Johnson in the films *Happy Birthday, Marsha!* by Tourmaline and *Pay It No Mind* by Michael Kasino. Sylvia Rivera was a life-long organizer who worked with many organizations including the Young Lords and Gay Liberation Front. She was an outspoken advocate for trans women of color to be included in the fight for gay liberation. This can be seen in her famous speech "Y'all better quiet down" at the Christopher Street Liberation Day in 1973.

Johnson & Rivera left an important legacy by resisting assimilation and focusing on housing access, fighting back against police, supporting queer youth and centering the needs of trans women of color. "City of Trans Liberation," p. 26 & afterword, p. 52.

Miss Major Griffin-Gracy is a Black transgender elder and activist who was born in Chicago in 1940. She moved to New York City and was an active force in the Stonewall Riots. Major is a survivor of Attica State Prison and a former sex worker. Her decades of activism across the country have been focused on advocating for trans women of color who are sex workers, survivors of police brutality, and who are currently or formerly incarcerated. She worked with the Trans, Gender-Variant and Intersex Justice Project, and her legacy project is the House of GG. You can learn more about Major in the films *The Personal Things* by Tourmaline and *MAJOR!* by Annalise Ophelian. "On Trans Street," p. 28.

Jennicet Gutiérrez is a transgender Latina from México who was born in 1986. She is an organizer with Familia: Trans Queer Liberation Movement. In 2015, Gutiérrez received national attention when she attended a pride event at the White House under then president Barack Obama. While he was giving a speech, she called on him from the crowd to release trans immigrants from detention centers and address the violence trans women face in detention. Reflecting on that day, she wrote, "There is no pride in how LGBTQ immigrants are treated in this country." She continues to amplify the voices of trans women of color and works to free immigrants and people of color from the carceral system. "Camp Trans," p. 33

V. RELATED WORK

Films
Disclosure by Sam Feder (2020)

Free CeCe by Laverne Cox and Jacques Gares (2016)

Happy Birthday, Marsha! by Tourmaline (2017)

MAJOR! by Annalise Ophelian (2015)

Paragraph 175 by Rob Epstein and Jeffrey Friedman (2000)

Pay It No Mind by Michael Kasino (2012)

Screaming Queens by Susan Stryker and Victor Silverman (2005)

We've Been Around series by Rhys Ernst (2016)

Books
Branded by the Pink Triangle by Ken Setterington

Captive Genders edited by Nat Smith & Eric A. Stanley

Care Work by Leah Lakshmi Piepzna-Samarasinha

Pet by Akwaeke Emezi

Sex is a Funny Word by Cory Silverberg

To Survive on This Shore by Jess T. Dugan & Vanessa Fabbre

Trans Care by Hil Malatino

Transgender History by Susan Stryker

We Both Laughed in Pleasure: The Selected Diaries of Lou Sullivan
edited by Ellis Martin & Zach Ozma

We Do This 'Til We Free Us by Mariame Kaba

Archives & Museums
The Digital Trans Archive
    https://www.digitaltransgenderarchive.net/

Gerber/Hart Library, Chicago, IL
    https://www.gerberhart.org/

GLBT Historical Society, San Francisco, CA
https://www.glbthistory.org

Illinois Holocaust Museum, Skokie, IL
https://www.ilholocaustmuseum.org/

Leather Archives & Museum, Chicago, IL
https://leatherarchives.org/

Lesbian Herstory Archives, Brooklyn, NY
https://lesbianherstoryarchives.org/

Leslie/Lohman Museum, New York City, NY
https://www.leslielohman.org/

Museum of Transgender Hirstory & Art
www.sfmotha.org

ONE Archives, Los Angeles, CA
https://www.onearchives.org

Queer Zine Archive Project
www.archive.qzap.org

Stonewall Museum & Archive, Ft. Lauderdale, FL
https://stonewall-museum.org/

Community Organizations

Below are a few organizations whose politics, organizing, and
programs have helped shape the vision of this book.

Black & Pink
https://blackandpinkpenpals.org/

Brave Space Alliance
https://www.bravespacealliance.org/

Chicago Women's Health Center
https://www.chicagowomenshealthcenter.org/

Dyke March Chicago
https://www.facebook.com/Dyke-MarchChicago/

Familia: Trans Queer Liberation Movement
https://familiatqlm.org/

Gay Shame
https://gayshame.net/

Lyon-Martin Health Services
https://www.healthright360.org/agency/lyon-martin-health-services

Masjid al-Rabia
https://masjidalrabia.org

Sylvia Rivera Law Project
https://www.srlp.org

TransLatin@ Coalition
https://www.translatinacoalition.org/

Transformative Justice Law Project
https://www.tjlp.org/

Visual AIDS
https://visualaids.org/

William Way LGBT Community Center
https://www.waygay.org/

NOTES

"City of Trans Liberation" is after Martín Espada's poem "Imagine the Angels of Bread."

"If You Are Over Cis People" is after Morgan Parker's poem "If You Are Over Staying Woke."

"At the Dream Job" is titled after Carmen Maria Machado's book *In the Dream House*.

"Trans Lit" is after Jamila Woods's poem "Blk Girl Art."

"There are Trans People Here" is after Jamaal May's poem "There Are Birds Here."

"Dysphoria Is Not My Name" is after Ross Gay's poem "Sorrow Is Not My Name." The italicized line is from this poem.

"To Sylvie, To Frank" is after Frank O'Hara's poem "Adieu to Norman, Bon Jour to Joan and Jean-Paul." The italicized line is from this poem.

"Trans Day of Revenge" is after the song of the same name by G.L.O.S.S.

ACKNOWLEDGMENTS

Some of the poems in this collection were included in the chapbook *On My Way to Liberation* (Haymarket Books, 2018). The following poems previously appeared in:

Chicago Reader: "At the Chicago Marathon" and "Prayer for My Trans Siblings"

Cosmonauts Avenue: "On Trans Street"

Heart Journal: "On My Way to Liberation"

Hooligan Mag: "Giovanni's Room" and "I Don't Want a Trans President"

Jewish Currents: "There are Trans People Here"

Lambda Literary: "City of Trans Liberation"

The Rumpus: "Trans Day of Revenge," and "All the Missing Sweetness"

Split This Rock: "Every Day is a Trans Day"

Tinderbox: "Intensive Care"

Vida Review: "Dysphoria Is Not My Name"

GRATITUDE TO

Nate Marshall. Jamila Woods. Fatimah Asghar. Eve Ewing. Alison C. Rollins. River Kerstetter. Oli Rodriguez. Reese Kelly. Sylvie Lydon. Ydalmi Noriega. Fred Sasaki. Emily Jungmin Yoon. Sam Herschel Wein. Levi Todd. Ruby Western. Shira Erlichman. Angel Nafis. Morgan Parker. Hanif Abdurraqib. Kaveh Akbar. Cameron Awkward-Rich. Franny Choi. Danez Smith. Eloisa Amezcua. José Olivarez. Britteney Black Rose Kapri. Logan Pierce. Patrick Del Percio. Tempestt Hazel. Krista Franklin. Kris Hankins. My parents. My therapist. My doctors. The Tin House Workshop. The team at Haymarket Books. Trans writers who write for us.

ABOUT THE AUTHOR

H. Melt is a poet, artist, and educator whose work celebrates trans people, history, and culture. They are the author of *The Plural, The Blurring* and editor of *Subject to Change: Trans Poetry & Conversation*. H. Melt was an artist-in-residence at the Newberry Library, researching the Chicago Protest Collection. They attended the Tin House Writer's Workshop and received the Judith A. Markowitz Award for Emerging LGBTQ Writers from Lambda Literary.

ABOUT HAYMARKET BOOKS

Haymarket Books is a radical, independent, nonprofit book publisher based in Chicago. Our mission is to publish books that contribute to struggles for social and economic justice. We strive to make our books a vibrant and organic part of social movements and the education and development of a critical, engaged, international left.

We take inspiration and courage from our namesakes, the Haymarket martyrs, who gave their lives fighting for a better world. Their 1886 struggle for the eight-hour day—which gave us May Day, the international workers' holiday—reminds workers around the world that ordinary people can organize and struggle for their own liberation. These struggles continue today across the globe—struggles against oppression, exploitation, poverty, and war.

Since our founding in 2001, Haymarket Books has published more than five hundred titles. Radically independent, we seek to drive a wedge into the risk-averse world of corporate book publishing. Our authors include Noam Chomsky, Arundhati Roy, Rebecca Solnit, Angela Y. Davis, Howard Zinn, Amy Goodman, Wallace Shawn, Mike Davis, Winona LaDuke, Ilan Pappé, Richard Wolff, Dave Zirin, Keeanga-Yamahtta Taylor, Nick Turse, Dahr Jamail, David Barsamian, Elizabeth Laird, Amira Hass, Mark Steel, Avi Lewis, Naomi Klein, and Neil Davidson. We are also the trade publishers of the acclaimed Historical Materialism Book Series and of Dispatch Books.

CPSIA information can be obtained
at www.ICGtesting.com
Printed in the USA
JSHW021030220122
22146JS00003B/13